DATE DUE

AUG 0 2 2005			
GAYLORD			PRINTED IN U.S.A.

The Library of
Turtles and Tortoises™

Green Sea Turtles

Christopher Blomquist

The Rosen Publishing Group's
PowerKids Press™
New York

For Carolyn, a friend to kith and creatures

Published in 2004 by The Rosen Publishing Group, Inc.
29 East 21st Street, New York, NY 10010

First Edition

Editor: Natashya Wilson
Book Design: Michael J. Caroleo

Photo Credits: Cover and title page © Digital Stock; p. 4 © Stuart Westmorland/CORBIS; pp. 7, 20 by Bradley/Ireland; pp. 8 (bottom), 11, 15, 19 © Victoria McCormick/Animals Animals; p. 12 (top left) © Stephen Frink/CORBIS; p. 16 © Len Osf/Zell/Animals Animals.

Blomquist, Christopher.
Green sea turtles / Christopher Blomquist.— 1st ed.
     v. cm. — (The library of turtles and tortoises)
Includes bibliographical references (p.   ).
Contents: The Gentle Green Giant — An Ocean-Loving Turtle — Keeping Warm — No Meat for Me! — Mating and Multiplying — Nesting Mothers — A Rough Childhood — Tired Turtles — Deadly Dangers — An Uncertain Future.
ISBN 0-8239-6738-7 (lib. bdg.)
1. Green turtle—Juvenile literature. [1. Green turtle. 2. Turtles. 3. Endangered species.] I. Title. II. Series.
QL666.C536 B62 2004
597.92'8—dc21
                                          2002154173

Manufactured in the United States of America

Contents

Carapace

Plastron

The Gentle Green Giant

The world's oceans are home to many different kinds of life, such as fish, seaweed, shellfish, and whales. Seven different **species**, or kinds, of turtles also live in the oceans. The green sea turtle is one of the largest of the hard-shelled turtles. When the green sea turtle is fully grown, its shell is from 2 ½ to 5 feet (.8–1.5 m) long. Adult green sea turtles are also heavy. They weigh from 250 to 450 pounds (113.4–204.1 kg). These turtles get their name from their green-colored body fat, not from the color of their shells. The **carapace**, or top of the shell, is brown or olive. The **plastron**, or bottom of the shell, is white or yellow. The turtle's tough skin is brown, gray, or black. Green sea turtles are gentle animals. Often, when they float at the water's surface, seabirds perch on their backs.

The bottom of the green sea turtle's shell is light colored. This makes it hard for enemies below the turtle to see it.

An Ocean-Loving Turtle

The green sea turtle is well built for its life in the ocean. Its head is small, and its two front legs are shaped like flippers. The shapes of the head and legs help the turtle to swim quickly. Green sea turtles can swim as far as 57 ⅘ miles (93 km) in one day.

All turtles belong to the group of animals called **reptiles**. As do all reptiles, a green sea turtle breathes with lungs and has scaly skin. The world's turtle population is made of both turtles and tortoises. Although all tortoises are turtles, not all turtles are tortoises. "Tortoise" is a common name for turtles that live only on land. Green sea turtles live mostly in the water. They are turtles, not tortoises.

A green sea turtle's front and back legs are flat and broad. They help the turtle to swim quickly and easily through the sea.

Green Sea Turtle Worldwide Range

Keeping Warm

Green sea turtles are usually found in warm, shallow water off coasts in the Atlantic, Pacific, and Indian Oceans. They are **cold-blooded** animals, which means that their body **temperature** is changed by air or water temperature. For this reason, most sea turtles live in **tropical** areas. However, green sea turtles have been spotted in places as far north as Massachusetts and Alaska. These turtles probably followed warm ocean currents up north.

During the day, green sea turtles climb out of the water onto beaches and rocky ledges to **bask** in the sunlight. Resting in the hot sun warms the turtles' blood. It also keeps them out of deep water during the time of day when sharks are likely to hunt them. Green sea turtles are the only sea turtles that bask.

Top: *Green sea turtles live in oceans within the orange area on this map.* Bottom: *These green sea turtles are basking on a beach in Hawaii. Basking green sea turtles may flip sand onto their shells.*

9

Food for Turtles

Adult green sea turtles eat mostly plants. These turtles' favorite foods are sea grasses that grow underwater near the shore, and **algae**, which includes different types of seaweed. Sometimes green sea turtles will eat small sea animals, but these turtles prefer eating plants. The sharp edges of the turtles' toothless jaws help them to tear up food. Baby green sea turtles eat both plants and animals, including worms, small shellfish, sponges, and sea insects. The meat in their diet helps them to grow faster. Newborn babies are from 1 ⅜ to 2 ⅜ inches (3.5–6 cm) long. When the turtles are from 8 to 10 inches (20–25 cm) long, or from 1 to 2 years old, they begin to eat less meat. Around this time, the turtle also picks a feeding range, the food-rich stretch of water that it will call home.

This adult female green sea turtle is eating a meal of sea plants. Her territory is in Hawaii.

Turtle and Tortoise Facts

Scientists believe that basking helps green sea turtles to get enough vitamin D, which isn't plentiful in plants. The sun reacts with matter in the turtles' skin to create vitamin D, which helps bones to grow.

Turtle and Tortoise Facts

How do you tell male and female green sea turtles apart? The males have longer tails!

Green Sea Turtle Migration Routes

Mating and Multiplying

One amazing thing about green sea turtles is how they **mate** and multiply. An adult turtle's home territory may be more than 1,000 miles (1,609 km) away from its birthplace. However, the turtle will swim all the way back to the waters by its birthplace, or **natal beach**, to produce its own offspring! It is believed that the turtles use Earth's magnetic field along with sounds, the Sun, and the stars to **migrate** back to these spots. In the United States, the turtles nest in Hawaii and eastern Florida.

Green sea turtles mate for the first time when they are between 19 and 24 years old. They mate in the water, about ½ mile (1 km) offshore. A male courts a female by nuzzling her head and nibbling on her neck and legs.

A male green sea turtle (top left) will fight other males to mate with a female (top right). Bottom: This map shows paths that green sea turtles are known to swim when migrating from their feeding grounds to their natal beaches and back.

Nesting Mothers

After mating, the female gets ready to lay a **clutch** of eggs. She leaves the water for a few hours at night to nest. Females come ashore during the cooler nighttime so that their heavy bodies won't overheat during the crawl in the sand. A mother turtle uses her legs to dig her nest in the sand. She lays usually from 100 to 120 soft, leathery-skinned eggs in the nest and covers them with sand. Then she returns to the ocean. She stays in the area for about two weeks. Then she comes ashore and nests again. A female may nest up to seven times during a five-month mating season. In that time she may lay more than 800 eggs! After nesting, the females need a few years of rest and food to get their bodies strong enough to nest again. For this reason, they mate and nest every two to four years.

Nests may be as deep as 2 ½ feet (76 cm). This female green sea turtle is covering her newly laid eggs with sand.

Turtle and Tortoise Facts

The temperature of the nest decides the sex of these turtles. Temperatures above 84.2°F (29°C) make more females. Temperatures below 84.2°F make more males.

A Rough Childhood

Many green sea turtle eggs are eaten by animals or humans. If the eggs do hatch, the baby turtles, or **hatchlings**, must take care of themselves. Depending on the nest location and the temperature, the eggs usually hatch after 50 to 55 days. Each hatchling uses its **egg tooth** to break through the shell. The hatchling then works its way out of the shell. Once out, hatchlings wait for the other hatchlings to break out of their shells. The hatchlings dig out of the nest together at night, when the sand is cool. Then they crawl toward the sea. Many hatchlings never make it to the water. **Predators** such as birds, snakes, and rats eat them on the shore. Others are eaten in the ocean by sharks, fish, and dolphins. Young green sea turtles spend their first three years eating and hiding in seaweed patches.

These baby green sea turtles hatched in Australia. Fewer than 1 in 1,000 green sea turtles lives from egg to adulthood.

Tired Turtles

Unlike many other turtles, most green sea turtles do not **hibernate**, because they live in areas that stay warm during the winter. However, these turtles do need their nightly rest. Adult turtles, which are active during the day, often sleep on the ocean floor or on rocky ledges above the water. The turtles close their nostrils while they sleep underwater. While active, the turtles come up to the surface every few minutes to breathe. While resting, they can stay underwater without coming up for as long as 13 hours. Their blood and muscles store enough oxygen to let them do this. Young turtles aren't big enough to store that much air, so they sleep while floating on top of the water.

This green sea turtle is resting on the ocean floor. At rest a green sea turtle's heart may beat just once every 9 minutes.

Turtle and Tortoise Facts

Green sea turtles appear to cry sometimes. They aren't upset, they are actually getting rid of extra salt through special glands behind their eyes!

Deadly Dangers

Green sea turtles can live long lives. Some scientists believe they can live to be up to 100 years old! However, green sea turtles face danger each day. Humans are the turtles' worst enemies. For hundreds of years, people have eaten green sea turtle meat and eggs. People still hunt these turtles for food, even in places where it is against the law. Fishing nets can also trap the turtles and cause them to drown. Some turtles die from eating pieces of plastic that people have dumped into the ocean. The building of beach houses and hotels has destroyed some of the turtles' nesting sites. A sickness called **fibropapilloma** has also killed many green sea turtles. This sickness causes wartlike growths to appear on the skin. Scientists are trying to find the cause of this deadly illness.

Many green sea turtle bones lie underwater in the Sipadan Caves in Malaysia. No one knows why turtles die in the caves.

An Uncertain Future

When Christopher Columbus landed in what are now the Cayman Islands in 1503, the islands had so many green sea turtles on them that they looked as if they were covered with rocks. Today that is no longer true, nor is it true of other places where the turtles once lived in great numbers. The green sea turtle is now an **endangered** species.

Countries such as the United States have passed laws to protect green sea turtles and their nesting grounds. In some parts of the world, the turtles are raised on turtle farms. Some are raised for their meat, and others are raised to be set free in the wild.

However, the green sea turtle's future is uncertain. Governments and turtle groups throughout the world must work together to save the species, so that this gentle green giant does not disappear from the oceans forever.

Glossary

algae (AL-jee) A plantlike living thing without roots or stems that lives in water.

bask (BASK) To lie in the sun.

carapace (KER-uh-pays) The upper part of a turtle's shell.

clutch (KLUCH) The group of eggs laid by a female animal at one time.

cold-blooded (KOHLD-bluh-did) Having a body heat that changes with the surrounding heat.

egg tooth (EG TOOTH) A sharp, toothlike part on a baby animal's beak, used to crack open the eggshell.

endangered (en-DAYN-jerd) In danger of no longer existing.

fibropapilloma (fy-broh-pa-pih-LOH-muh) A sickness that causes wartlike growths on the soft parts of a turtle's body.

hatchlings (HACH-lingz) Baby animals that have just come out of their eggs.

hibernate (HY-bur-nayt) To spend the winter in a sleeplike state.

mate (MAYT) To join together to make babies.

migrate (MY-grayt) To move from one place to another.

natal beach (NAY-tul BEECH) The beach where a sea turtle was born.

plastron (PLAS-tron) The bottom, flatter part of a turtle's shell that covers the belly.

predators (PREH-duh-terz) Animals that kill other animals for food.

reptiles (REP-tylz) Cold-blooded animals with lungs and scales.

species (SPEE-sheez) A single kind of living thing.

temperature (TEM-pruh-chur) How hot or cold something is.

tropical (TRAH-puh-kul) Having to do with the warm parts of Earth that are near the equator.

Index

Web Sites

Due to the changing nature of Internet links, PowerKids Press has developed an online list of Web sites related to the subject of this book. This site is updated regularly. Please use this link to access the list:
www.powerkidslinks.com/ltt/greensea/